Spring H~~a~~
Bible Workbook

MISSION

Connect!
Finding your place

Peter Brierley and Tim Jeffery

LIFESTYLE

Equipping the Church for action

First published in 2003 Spring Harvest Publishing Division and Authentic Lifestyle

09 08 07 06 05 04 03   7 6 5 4 3 2 1

Authentic Lifestyle is an imprint of Authentic Media

PO Box 300, Carlisle, Cumbria, CA3 0QS, UK

and Box 1047, Waynesboro, GA 30830-2047, USA

www.paternoster-publishing.com

British Library Cataloguing in Publication Data

A catalogue record for this book is available from the British Library

ISBN 1-85078-521-X

Typeset by Spring Harvest
Cover design by Diane Bainbridge
Printed in Great Britain by Bell and Bain Ltd., Glasgow

CONTENTS

ABOUT THIS BOOK

This study book aims to help you consider what mission is and how we can be most effective as missionaries, given the culture we are a part of. It does not concentrate on a particular book of the Bible but uses a variety of passages as a springboard into discussing our theme.

▶ The emphasis of the studies will be on the application of the Bible. You will be encouraged to think 'How does this apply to me? How does this apply to our church? What can we do to make our mission more dynamic, more biblical?'

▶ House groups can encourage honesty and make space for questions and doubts. The aim of the studies is not to find the right answer, but to help the members understand the Bible and understand what mission is by working through their questions. Of course there will be differences of opinion but the housegroup should be a safe place to express honestly what you think and feel. The important thing is to be open to learning new ways of doing mission and being a missionary.

▶ Housegroups can give opportunities for deep friendships to develop. Group members will be encouraged to talk about their experiences, feelings, questions, hopes and fears. They will be able to offer one another pastoral support and to get involved in each other's lives.

▶ There is a difference between being a collection of individuals who happen to meet together every Wednesday and being an effective group who bounce ideas off each other, spark inspiration and creativity, pooling their talents and resources to create solutions together: one whose whole is definitely greater than the sum of its parts. The process of working through these studies will encourage healthy group dynamics.

Space is given for you to write answers, comments, questions and thoughts. This book will not tell you what to think, but will help you discover the truth of God's word through thinking, discussing, praying and listening.

FOR GROUP MEMBERS

- You will probably get more out of the study if you spend some time during the week reading the passage and thinking about the questions. Make a note of anything you don't understand.

- Pray that God will help you to understand the passage and show you how to apply it. Pray for other members in the group, too, that they will find the study helpful.

- Be willing to take part in the discussions. The leader of the group is not there as an expert with all the answers. They will want everyone to get involved and share their thoughts and opinions.

- However, don't dominate the group! If you are aware that you are saying a lot, make space for others to contribute. Be sensitive to other group members and aim to be encouraging. If you disagree with someone, say so but without putting down their contribution.

FOR INDIVIDUALS

- Although this book is written with a group in mind, it can also be easily used by individuals. You obviously won't be able to do the group activities suggested, but you can consider how you would answer the questions and write your thoughts in the space provided.

- You may find it helpful to talk to a prayer partner about what you have learnt, and ask them to pray for you as you try and apply what you are learning to your life.

- The New International Version of the text is printed in the book. If you use a different version, then read from your own Bible as well.

INTRODUCTION

'The Church exists by mission as fire exists by burning.' In other words, mission is central to everything that the Church is and does. For most Christians, however, mission is something that other people do – people who work for mission organisations, the people we give money to once a month by direct debit. Jesus said 'As the Father has sent me, I am sending you', but how many of us take the 'you' in Jesus' statement and apply it to ourselves: individually, as a small group, and as a local church? The studies in this book, inspired by the *Connect!* book by Tim Jeffery and Steve Chalke, are designed to help you think about your response to Jesus' question and the role he is calling you to in his global mission.

As the world changes, we are presented with new ways of doing mission. Opportunities abound, but how should we react to the opportunities that have arisen in our ever-changing culture? Is it right to change our mission methods when we have done it in the same way for so long? These are some of the questions we need to look at in order to engage with mission in an appropriate way.

The central theme of the Bible is God's mission to the world and man's involvement in it. Wherever you turn in the Bible there is something to be learnt about mission. For this reason, these studies are not based on any particular book of the Bible. Instead, we draw from the Bible's rich teaching on this topic and seek to base our convictions about mission on the foundations of his word.

We hope that everyone that interacts with the Bible studies in this booklet will be challenged to see mission in new and exciting ways. May you be inspired and begin to explore new ways in which you can get involved. Our prayer is that the outcome of following these studies will not just be ideas, but action.

THE WORLD IS SHRINKING FAST!

Aim: To understand what globalisation is, and to see how it might benefit the way we think about and do global mission

Tom plans to holiday in Thailand this summer and has just come back from visiting friends in China. He has an American girlfriend, and enjoys chatting to her family on the internet. His favourite hobby is eating. He particularly likes the variety that he can get near his workplace on London's Oxford Street: Chinese, Indian, Mexican, American, Thai and Greek – you name it, he can get it!!

Fifty years ago, many of these things in Tom's life wouldn't have been possible, but with the changes we have seen in technology and communication, our lives have been opened up to many more opportunities. Cultures, countries and people are becoming more interconnected and more interdependent. This process is called globalisation and, believe it or not, it affects the way we do mission.

> *Then the eleven disciples went to Galilee, to the mountain where Jesus had told them to go. When they saw him, they worshipped him; but some doubted. Then Jesus came to them and said, 'All authority in heaven and on earth has been given to me. Therefore go and make disciples of all nations, baptising them in the name of the Father and of the Son and of the Holy Spirit, and teaching them to obey everything I have commanded you. And surely I am with you always, to the very end of the age.*
>
> *Matthew 28:16–20*

TO SET THE SCENE

Get yourself a map of the world and ask everybody to put a sticker on the places where they have contacts or family, places they have been on holiday or visited on business. Include any places where people linked to your church are working in mission. Are the results of this activity a surprise to you?

READ MARK 16:15, MATTHEW 28:19

These commands must have been quite something to the eleven men Jesus addressed, most of whom would never have travelled much further than Jerusalem in the course of their lives. It becomes apparent from the New Testament's accounts

of all the missionary journeys that Jesus was literally talking about the *whole* world, even though the disciples only went to the known world at that time. Jesus' command seems much more realistic to a generation who have connections with people all over the world.

1 When Jesus gave this command, did he expect each one of us to become full-time overseas missionaries? Do you think there is still a role for long-term missionaries from Western countries to other countries? Explain your answer.

2 Given the world we now live in, is long-term mission, as we have known it for the last two hundred years, the only effective way of doing mission? What other alternatives are you aware of?

3 What do you see as being your role in the task of global mission as individuals and as a church community?

4 Do you think the impact of globalisation is changing your understanding of what your role is?

5 In what other ways has globalisation affected the spread of the gospel?

READ NUMBERS 13:26–14:9

DO YOU WANT TO GO BACK TO EGYPT?

Globalisation may mean a transformation in the way we do mission. Changing the way we do things can be hard and painful. Israel learned this in its time in the wilderness. The Bible presents us with two perspectives we might adopt regarding the future, one is to be positive, to look for opportunities, which demonstrate that we are a people of hope. The other is to become cynical about change and nostalgic about the past, both of which lead to paralysis and defeat.

6 Read the text again and make a note of the differences between Caleb and Joshua's responses and that of the majority of the Israelite community.

7 We are living in a critical period of history. The choices we make as Christians now will affect what God's church in our country will look like and how it does mission for the next century. Are you someone who finds change easy or hard?

8 Would you naturally respond like Caleb and Joshua or the majority of the Israelites?

Taken as a whole, globalisation is not, of itself, only good or bad. What people decide to do with the opportunities it presents can be. The question for Christians is, will we harness its power and use it for the furtherance of God's kingdom?

IT IS POSSIBLE!
Here is an example of the way one church has made the most of globalisation.

> Bournemouth Family Church (BFC) undertakes its own global mission activities. It has strong links with groups of churches in two areas of Uganda, and teams from BFC pay regular visits there, sometimes staying for several weeks. One leader took out his whole family to live with the local people for a while. BFC members undertake preaching and training but also health care, setting up schools and sponsoring some children who attend them, and promoting self-support projects for local pastors. In addition they are working with one of the Ugandan church groupings, with support from Wycliffe Bible translators, to evangelise and church-plant among an unreached people in a nearby country.

WORSHIP

Using your map, pray for some of the links you have and thank God that we are a part of one great global family.

DURING THE WEEK

Classically, world mission has been from the West to the rest. In an interconnected, globalised world we can begin to appreciate that we might have something to learn from other countries. Start to think about which countries your church could learn from (perhaps ones that you have mentioned you have a link with).

Read Chapter 1 of *Connect!* by Tim Jeffery and Steve Chalke for a more in-depth discussion on globalisation, as well as suggestions for further study.

MISSION IN TRANSITION

Aim: To explore how our culture affects the way we do mission

TO SET THE SCENE
Discuss, in groups of three or four, some significant transitions in your life: from school to university, a change in career, moving from one country or culture to another.

How did it feel? What thought processes did you go through? What were the emotional effects? Was it easy or was it hard? Did it make you see what you had left behind in a different light?

REFLECT
Every so often a whole society can undergo a fundamental change of culture or worldview, when its most basic assumptions will be questioned. As this happens, we often realise that what we thought was normal or obviously true is, in fact, just one way of looking at an issue. You see this on a small scale when you travel abroad and see various things being done totally differently.

The early church faced a massive transition when the spread of the gospel to non-Jews forced the church's leaders, themselves of Jewish background, to consider how much of their heritage was actually essential to salvation, and how much was simply tradition.

> *Culture* All societies have 'cultures', as do most groups, organisations, and even families. Culture is made up of a collection of generally accepted attitudes, basic assumptions, stories, heroes and villains. It has been summed up by one writer as 'the way we do things round here'.

READ ACTS 15

1 What dilemma was the early church facing here? (Acts 15:1–2)

2 Why was this difficult for them?

3 What decision did the council take, and why? (Acts 15:6–20)

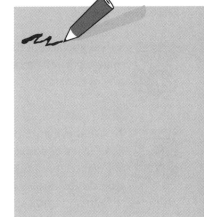

4 To what extent did their own cultural background influence the thinking and the decision of those attending the council? (Acts 15:1,20)

HOW DOES THIS **5** What can we learn from the council's decision and how they dealt with the situation?

APPLY TO ME

We are living at a time when a lot of the basic assumptions about life and how we live it are being radically questioned. All of the evidence points to the fact that our society is undergoing a massive transition. It is a transition from what is called 'modernity' to 'postmodernity'.

INDIVIDUAL ACTIVITY
The exercise below is to allow you to explore how modern/postmodern your thinking is. Younger generations tend to be more influenced by postmodernity. Read the pairs of sentences. The line below each pair acts as a scale. Put a mark on the scale at a point where you are most happy:

Modern	Postmodern
Truth is fixed and absolute	Truth unfolds and is a journey rather than a destination
Reason is the only way to discover truth	Reason is one way of discovering truth, I use my experience and intuition too
I believe in the importance of orthodoxy and conforming to the norms of society	I believe in diversity and listening to minority voices
Long-term planning, and a commitment to a job for life is preferable	I am comfortable with change, and would prefer to experience lots of different jobs rather than just one
I am most comfortable in structured settings and in organisations where everyone's role is clearly defined	I like an informal and unstructured environment centred on relationships and networks

DISCUSS

6 Do you accept that our society is changing from a modern to a postmodern way of thinking?

7 What evidence do you see for the differences described above? Think about popular culture (media, music, heroes); attitudes to careers and commitments; attitudes to faith and truth; standards of behaviour or dress; attitudes to differences in race, religion, and sexuality.

8 How as Christians are we affected by these changes or do we stand apart from them?

9 In what ways do you think postmodernity is already changing the way we do and think about global mission, or is likely to change them in the future? Think about evangelism to those of other faiths; the length of time people commit to mission; views on what mission is, etc...

DON'T BE AN OSTRICH!

Transitions are always hard, as you probably recognised when you started this session. However, we cannot bury our heads (like the ostrich) and pretend that change is not happening. If the early Christians hadn't made the effort to understand and respond to what God was doing through the spread of the gospel to non-Jews, then Christianity might have remained an offshoot of Judaism. The changes our society is undergoing now are cultural, but they too challenge us to review our understanding of what the gospel *actually* says about mission and what are essentially cultural attitudes and traditions.

> *The legacy of the past pushes us in a certain direction, which is to create more of the same. The easy path is to move continually in the same line, opting for what is familiar and safe. But among the range of possibilities which confronts us there will be one that represents the divine lure to go against convention and to make something radically new of ourselves and our world.*[1]

WORSHIP

Write down on a large piece of paper the things in our culture that we can be thankful for. Does your worship before God need to be a time of repentance for being pessimistic about the future?

DURING THE WEEK

Look for signs of postmodernity around you and continue to think about which parts of our Christianity are cultural expressions as opposed to biblical truths. Write them down and bring them to the group for the next session.

The words postmodernism and postmodernity are on the lips of so many people. If you want to find out some more about their meaning and significance, read *Connect!*, Chapter Two.

1. *The Sacred Journey* by Mike Riddell, (Oxford: Lion Publishing Plc, 2000) p103

MORE TO MISSION THAN MEETS THE EYE

Aim: To look more closely at what mission is

This session is not for the fainthearted. It may challenge and question your presuppositions but hopefully you will leave the session with a broader understanding of mission.

> *[Jesus] went to Nazareth, where he had been brought up, and on the Sabbath day he went into the synagogue, as was his custom. And he stood up to read. The scroll of the prophet Isaiah was handed to him. Unrolling it, he found the place where it is written:*
>
> *'The Spirit of the Lord is on me, because he has anointed me to preach good news to the poor. He has sent me to proclaim freedom for the prisoners and recovery of sight for the blind, to release the oppressed, to proclaim the year of the Lord's favour.'*
>
> *Then he rolled up the scroll, gave it back to the attendant and sat down. The eyes of everyone in the synagogue were fastened on him, and he began by saying to them, 'Today this scripture is fulfilled in your hearing.'*
>
> ***Luke 4:16–21***

TO SET THE SCENE

Look at the list below and discuss amongst yourselves which points should be part of our understanding of mission and which should not:

- Teaching from the Bible
- Feeding the hungry
- Preaching
- Writing to governments to set innocent people free from prison
- Teaching people life skills
- Giving people money
- The relief of suffering
- Evangelistic talks
- Church-planting

Having looked at the list and decided which ones you consider to be valid parts of mission, discuss whether you would give priority to any one dimension over and against the others.

READ ISAIAH 58, MICAH 6:8

WHAT DOES SEARCH THE BIBLE SAY?

1 Isaiah 58:6–12 describes what could be understood as the mandate for Israel's way of living. Do these instructions shed any light on what it means to be a mission-minded Christian in today's world?

ENGAGING WITH THE WORLD

2 From both of these passages we see that justice is a significant theme in the Old Testament. As Christians, do you think we focus enough on issues of justice today?

READ LUKE 4:14-20, MATTHEW 25:31-46, JAMES 2:14-26

WHAT DOES SEARCH THE BIBLE SAY?

3 Do you think the New Testament continues the theme of justice, and how much should this be a part of our understanding of mission?

4   Having read and reflected on these passages, would you now approach the list at the beginning of this session any differently?

REFLECT
Which of these statements do you think would be nearest to Jesus' understanding of what mission is? Discuss what you think about each statement.

> *The mission of the church is evangelism alone.*
> **Arthur Johnston**[1]

> *Mission is about bringing shalom to people. Occurring more than two hundred and fifty times in the Old Testament, shalom covers well-being in the widest sense of the word, incorporating notions of contentment, health, prosperity, justice, unity and salvation – at individual, communal, national, international, and creational levels.*
> **Dr Roger Hurding**[2]

1. *Battle For World Evangelism* (Wheaton: Tyndale, 1978)
2. *Pathways To Wholeness* (London: Hodder & Stoughton, 1998)

WORSHIP

Suggestion for worship song: *Beauty for brokenness.*[1]

Put a large piece of paper in the middle of the room and give everybody marker pens so that they can write down anything that they feel God is saying, and then reflect on it throughout the week. Sometimes we think in pictures and if a particular picture comes into your mind, try and draw it on the page.

▶ Part of our worship to God is sharing our grief for the struggling world around us. Ask him to show you how you can bring relief to those you know who are having difficulties.

▶ If you have a particular passion for the poor, the outcast, or the imprisoned ask God to change that passion from a spark to a flame.

▶ Thank God that he is a God who seeks justice for humankind.

DURING THE WEEK

If God has spoken to you about anything continue to pray and think about it throughout the week. If you have time, look at Simon Johnston and Steve Chalke's book *Intimacy and Involvement*, published by Kingsway Communications; ISBN: 184291118X.

1. Graham Kendrick - Spark to a Flame (1993), published by MakeWay Music

ME A MISSIONARY?

 Aim: To help you understand your identity as a global Christian and explore how you can use your personal interests, gifting and passion in God's global mission.

For years we have thought of missionaries as being those courageous (and often slightly eccentric) people who travel overseas doing Christian work. World mission has been seen as the job of mission agencies who are, after all, the professionals at it. We are called to love and serve our neighbours here at home, whilst they serve those further afield.

SET THE SCENE

▶ In your group discuss your reaction to this understanding. Has this been the way you have thought about mission?

Helen Kemble-Taylor is a nurse who has worked in the Accident and Emergency department in Southampton Hospital for about two years, bringing love and practical care to all the patients that she meets. Helen speaks of the growing realisation that, while God has been using her through the role, he was perhaps calling her to a wider vision, one of using her practical skills to change the lives of many, not just in Southampton, but throughout the world – in particular those countries where they lack the skills to provide good medical support. She now says she understands more fully what it means for God to love the whole world and not just her home territory.

In a globalised world, it is easier to have a real involvement in the 'world'. Our neighbour is no longer simply the person we live next door to but anyone, wherever they are in the world, on whom our life has an effect.

DISCUSS

HOW DOES THIS APPLY TO ME

1 To what extent do you see yourself as a missionary, and a global Christian?

ENGAGING WITH THE WORLD

2 What things might you be able to do to help a neighbour on the other side of the world? Have a look at the diagram that suggests some ways of starting to become a better global Christian and see if you could take any of the suggestions on board.

- Buy fairly traded products that ensure producers get a decent slice.

- Campaign for trade justice. Raise awareness in your church and write to your MP.

- Read the world news and pray for world leaders (1 Tim. 2: 1,2).

- Encourage people you know who are actively involved in mission by writing or visiting, as well as praying.

- Buy a copy of *The Good Shopping Guide* and consult it when you are going to buy something.

- Buy *Operation World* and read it, and pray about countries in which you have an interest.

- Consider working with a Christian mission organisation in the UK, either paid or as a volunteer.

- Where are you investing your money? Look at your bank accounts, savings and shares – could you find a more ethical home for them?

- If you travel abroad on business or holiday, find out about the churches in the places you visit and see what you could to to help them.

Becoming a global Christian

Some practical ideas to get you thinking

We [all] have different gifts, according to the grace given us. If a man's gift is prophesying, let him use it in proportion to his faith. If it is serving, let him serve; if it is teaching, let him teach; if it is encouraging, let him encourage; if it is contributing to the needs of others, let him give generously; if it is leadership, let him govern diligently; if it is showing mercy, let him do it cheerfully.

Romans 12:6–8

It was he who gave some to be apostles, some to be prophets, some to be evangelists, and some to be pastors and teachers...

Ephesians 4:11

Each one should use whatever gift he has received to serve others, faithfully administering God's grace in its various forms.

1 Peter 4:10

3   Read the above passages and then encourage each other... God made us all differently. We have different abilities, skills, gifting and interests. This wonderful diversity is his gift to us. Encourage one another by identifying at least one key strength or gift of each member of the group.

4   How could you use your gifts to get more involved as a global Christian? Start with who you are, what you are good at and what you like doing and see this as a way into your mission. For Helen, although not employed by a mission agency, her work is her mission, revealing God's love through her practical care. It is these skills that Helen can use to change dramatically the lives of people deprived of the basic medical skills we take for granted in this country.

Don't ask yourself what the world needs. Ask yourself what makes you come alive, and go do that, because what the world needs is people who have come alive.

Gil Bailie

WORSHIP

▶ Many of us are prevented from serving God because we don't believe that we are good enough. Remind yourself that your security does not come from your own strength but the strength that comes from Christ.

▶ There is something powerful about reading truth together. As a group, read 2 Corinthians 9–10 out loud.

▶ In twos, thank God for one another, giving thanks for the gifts God has given whoever you are praying with. Pray that God will encourage your neighbour to use their gifts and that he will help them to realise their potential.

DURING THE WEEK

Continue to think about what it is that makes you come alive, and pray about how you might be able to integrate that into your mission. Read Chapters 5,6,and 8 of *Connect!* to give you some more inspiration.

PREPARATION FOR THE NEXT SESSION

During the next session, we suggest that you have a meal together and each bring something to share. Try to organise yourselves so that you have dishes from as many different parts of the world as possible.

THE GLOBAL BODY

Aim: To see that Christians in the West are part of a global church and need Christians in other parts of the world

At the end of the last session we suggested that this week you should have a meal together, containing dishes from several countries or regions of the world. You can discuss the questions below while eating.

Your meal should be a rich mix of various smells and tastes from around the world. No doubt you could learn a lot from the way each country cooks a meal; each is different. In the last session we saw that every individual has something different to contribute to mission. Today we are thinking about the fact that each country and each church has something different to bring to the mission table. Each must be tasted, valued, and learned from.

> *The body is a unit, though it is made up of many parts; and though all its parts are many, they form one body. So it is with Christ. For we were all baptised by one Spirit into one body – whether Jews or Greeks, slave or free – and we were all given the one Spirit to drink.*
>
> *Now the body is not made up of one part but of many. If the foot should say, 'Because I am not a hand, I do not belong to the body,' it would not for that reason cease to be a part of the body. And if the ear should say 'Because I am not an eye, I do not belong to the body,' it would not for that reason cease to be a part of the body. If the whole body were an eye, where would the sense of hearing be? If the whole body were an ear, where would the sense of smell be? But in fact God has arranged the parts in the body, every one of them, just as he wanted them to be. If they were all one part, where would the body be? As it is there are many parts, but one body.*
>
> *The eye cannot say to the hand 'I don't need you!' And the head cannot say to the feet, 'I don't need you!' On the contrary, those parts of the body that seem to be weaker are indispensable, and the parts that we think are less*

honourable we treat with special honour. And the parts that are unpresentable are treated with special modesty, while our presentable parts need no special treatment. But God has combined the members of the body and has given greater honour to the parts that lacked it, so that there should be no division in the body, but that its parts should have equal concern for each other. If one part suffers, every part suffers with it; if one part is honoured, every part rejoices with it.

1 Corinthians 12:12–26

TO SET THE SCENE

Discuss what experience or contact you have had with Christians from other countries. Did you notice any special characteristics about their faith or the way they expressed it, that seemed typical of their nationality or region? Did they challenge or encourage your own faith?

READ 1 CORINTHIANS 12:12–26

WHAT DOES THE BIBLE SAY?

1 What does this passage teach us about working together?

2 Although this passage is specifically referring to the church of Corinth, in what ways could it be applied to the church globally?

3 To what extent does the global church feel like one body at present? For example, how far does the western church identify with, and support, Christians in other countries who are persecuted for their faith, or suffering acute poverty and deprivation?

4 The church in the West has been accused of arrogance: why do you think this is, and is it fair? If so, how could we change our attitudes and the perception of others?

5 Brainstorm. What could you or your church do to become a more active part of the global body of Christ?

I DON'T NEED YOU?

Christianity once thrived in the West. Because of our wealth and resources we saw ourselves as the primary provider of missionaries. It's been said that we need to give up seeing ourselves as the teacher and recognise the need to receive and be taught. Mission is no longer 'the West to the rest' but rather 'everywhere to everywhere'. So perhaps we should start to think of there being multiple centres of Christian influence, making up a network of mutual exchange and support.

> *The bottom line is that we need each other – we like to think we don't, but we're wrong. None of us on our own can understand it all, be it all, do it all – God deliberately made us interdependent.*
> **Tim Jeffery with Steve Chalke**[1]

DISCUSS

6 What do you see as the major areas of weakness in your own church, or in the Christian church nationally (e.g. outreach, prayer, passion for the Gospel, materialism)? Do you think that Christians in other parts of the world could help you on these? If so, how?

7 Looking at the chart over the page of the different strengths of the various parts of the global church (taken from *Connect!*), which part of the world do you think has most to offer your local church or the UK church more generally?

1. *Connect!* by Tim Jeffery with Steve Chalke, (Carlisle: Spring Harvest/ Authentic Publishing, 2003)

SESSION 5

The West	History/experience, teaching/training
China	Evangelistic zeal, experience of suffering
Africa	Community, spiritual gifts, hospitality, relational approach
Latin America	Community, vibrant faith, hospitality, prayer, passion for evangelism
India	Time for people, hospitality, prayer and fasting, evangelistic zeal
Eastern Europe	Experience of suffering, wholehearted commitment

IT IS POSSIBLE!

Glebe Farm Baptist Church has around twenty members and is situated in a poor area of Birmingham. However, it has built strong links with a large church in Brazil, and what it has learnt from the Brazilians about relationships has helped to transform the way the congregation relate to each other.

In addition, the 'cluster' of small churches in the area to which Glebe Farm belongs has been joined by a South Korean pastor whose vision, prayer life and passion for the gospel have all been a revelation to the Birmingham churches. Links have been established with his sending agency in South Korea and visits have taken place in both directions.

In what ways can you imagine your church learning from Christians from other parts of the world?

WORSHIP

Read Revelation 7:9–12 out loud.

▶ Thank God that he chooses people from every nation, tribe and language to be involved in mission.
▶ Thank God for being part of a global body.
▶ Praise him for the diversity of his creation.
▶ Ask that he will take the gifts of your church and the gifts of the global church and use them for the glory of his Kingdom.

FOR NEXT WEEK

In the session on globalisation you thought about the various countries that your group had connections with and you also began to think about which countries you might be able to learn from. Take some time out this week to be more specific in your exploration. If you know of particular churches ring them, email, or write to them and find out a bit more about them. Where are they weak and where are they strong? For more ideas and information, read *Connect!* chapters 3 and 6.

SUMMING UP – ALL MOUTH, NO MISSION?

Aim: To reflect on how your views on mission have changed since session 1, and to move from ideas to a plan of action

TO SET THE SCENE

As a group, use your bodies and get into a shape that you think represents the church. For example, would you be holding hands, standing close or far apart? If you don't feel comfortable doing this exercise, then describe how you might position people.

In a lot of cases, groups gather in a huddle and face inwards. This feels comfortable and safe, but it isn't how the church is called to be. Your group would far better represent church by holding hands and facing outwards. The church that remains inward looking remains stagnant; certainly there are times for intimacy but we must seek to be involved too.

This series of studies has been seeking to challenge your understanding of mission. We are all missionaries, and it is important that we recognise the massive potential that each of us, individually and in our churches, has for being actively involved in mission. You can have all the understanding and ideas in the world but if you don't take that brave step of faith then your church will remain one of many that has a mouth but is never heard beyond its own four walls; that has arms but never chooses to use them.

READ MATTHEW 14:22–33

1   Is Peter right to take the initiative in this act of faith? Or is he being presumptuous?

HOW DOES THIS   **2**   Imagine yourself in the boat – would you be as bold as Peter? Are you a risk-taker? Are you sometimes too reckless – or too cautious?

APPLY TO ME

3 What happens when Peter starts to sink? Does God always rescue us immediately we get into difficulties? If not, why do you think that is?

4 What does this passage remind us about God?

5 Have you ever tried anything and failed? Has failing spurred you on to try again, or has it made you give up?

Some things that your church tries may initially fail but don't give up. It is better to be a follower that fails than one who fails to follow at all!

REFLECT

6 In the first session, we asked you if you felt long-term mission was the only effective way of doing mission. How, if it all, has your answer to this changed?

APPLY THIS TO MY CHURCH

7 We also asked what you felt your role in mission as a church and as an individual was. Has your answer to this question changed and if so, in what ways?

ACTIVITY

Imagine that your church really stepped out of the boat and got involved in global mission. What might this look like in five years' time? Dream together about a time when your church is really taking God's global mission seriously and getting involved in ways that make sense with who you are and what interests you.

How can you begin to get the rest of your church enthused and interested in global mission? In coming up with a mission strategy, it is good to start by evaluating your situation. If your church's involvement in global mission is to be owned by a large proportion of the people, it has to interest and excite *them*. Think about how you could go about this.

Maybe you could plan a time when you can share your ideas with the whole church. If other small groups have been working through this booklet, pool all of your ideas and share your thoughts together.

Make sure ways are found that allow everybody's voice to be heard, not just your group's. You can use Chapter 9 of *Connect!* to help you develop your mission strategy.

BE BOLD, STEP OUT OF THE BOAT!

The boat is the place of comfort but it's not the place where we see miracles happening. You never know what you can do with God's strength until you step out in faith. Who would have thought Peter could have walked on water? Whatever you choose to do with your new understanding of mission; go boldly, knowing that great things can happen. Not everything you do will go according to plan, and not everything will work. Remember you need to find what is right for your church, given the resources, connections and passions you have.

> *Even the smallest person [or Church] can change the course of the future.*
> **Galadriel,** *The Lord of the Rings*

WORSHIP

Suggestion for worship song: *Let Your Glory Fall (Father of Creation).*[1]

▶ Pray about how you can help your whole church become involved in God's global mission.
▶ Ask that God will fill you afresh with his Spirit so that you, like Peter, might have boldness that comes from God.
▶ Worship is enriched by silence. Have a time of quiet where you allow God to speak to you.

LEADERS' GUIDE

TO HELP YOU LEAD

You may have led a housegroup many times before or this may be your first time. Here is some advice on how to lead these studies:

▶ As a group leader, you don't have to be an expert or a lecturer. You are there to facilitate the learning of the group members – helping them to discover for themselves the wisdom in God's word. You should not be doing most of the talking or dishing out the answers, whatever the group expects from you!

▶ You do need to be aware of the group's dynamics, however. People can be quite quick to label themselves and each other in a group situation. One person might be seen as the expert, another the moaner who always has something to complain about. One person may be labelled as quiet and not be expected to contribute; another person may always jump in with something to say. Be aware of the different type of individuals in the group, but don't allow the labels to stick. You may need to encourage those who find it hard to get a word in, and quieten down those who always have something to say. Talk to members between sessions to find out how they feel about the group.

▶ The sessions are planned to try and engage every member in active learning. Of course you cannot force anyone to take part if they don't want to, but it won't be too easy to be a spectator. Activities that ask everyone to write down a word or talk in twos, and then report back to the group, are there for a reason. They give everyone space to think and form their opinions, even if not everyone voices them out loud.

▶ Do adapt the sessions for your group as you feel is appropriate. Some groups may know each other very well and will be prepared to talk at a deep level. New groups may take a bit of time to get to know each other before making themselves vulnerable, but encourage members to share their lives with each other.

▶ You probably won't be able to tackle all the questions in each session so decide in advance which ones are most appropriate to your group and situation.

▶ Encourage a number of replies to each question. The study is not about finding a single right answer, but about sharing experiences and thoughts in order to find out how to apply the Bible to people's lives. When brainstorming, don't be too quick to evaluate the contributions. Write everything down and then have a look to see which suggestions are worth keeping.

▶ Similarly, encourage everyone to ask questions, voice doubts and discuss difficulties. Some parts of the Bible are difficult to understand. Sometimes the Christian faith throws up paradoxes. Painful things happen to us that make it difficult to see what God is doing. A housegroup should be a safe place to express all of this. If discussion doesn't resolve the issue, send everyone away to pray about it between sessions, and ask your minister for advice.

▶ Give yourself time in the week to read through the Bible passage and the questions. Read the Leaders' notes for the session, as different ways of presenting the questions are sometimes suggested. However, during the session don't be too quick to come in with the answer – sometimes people need space to think.

▶ Delegate as much as you like! The easiest activities to delegate are reading the text, and the worship sessions, but there are other ways to involve the group members. Giving people responsibility can help them own the session much more.

▶ Pray for group members by name, that God would meet with them during the week. Pray for the group session, for a constructive and helpful time. Ask the Lord to equip you as you lead the group.

THE STRUCTURE OF EACH SESSION

Feedback: find out what people remember from the previous session, or if they have been able to act during the week on what was discussed last time.

To set the scene: an activity or a question to get everyone thinking about the subject to be studied.

Bible reading: it's important actually to read the passage you are studying during the session. Ask someone to prepare this in advance or go around the group reading a verse or two each. Don't assume everyone will be happy to read out loud.

Questions and activities: adapt these as appropriate to your group. Some groups may enjoy a more activity-based approach; some may prefer just to discuss the questions. Try out some new things!

Worship: suggestions for creative worship and prayer are included, which give everyone an opportunity to respond to God, largely individually. Use these alongside singing or other group expressions of worship. Add a prayer time with opportunities to pray for group members and their families and friends.

For next week: this gives a specific task to do during the week, helping people to continue to think about or apply what they have learned.

Further study: suggestions are given for those people who want to study the themes further. These could be included in the housegroup if you feel it's appropriate and if there is time.

WHAT YOU NEED

A list of materials that are needed is printed at the start of each session in the Leaders' Guide. In addition you will probably need:

Bibles: the main Bible passage is printed in the book so that all the members can work from the same version. It is useful to have other Bibles available, or to ask everyone to bring their own, so that other passages can be referred to.

Paper and pens: for people who need more space than is in the book!

Flip chart: it is helpful to write down people's comments during a brainstorming session, so that none of the suggestions is lost. They may not be space for a proper flip chart in the average lounge, and having one may make it feel too much like a business meeting or lecture. Try getting someone to write on a big sheet of paper on the floor or coffee table, and then stick this up on the wall with blu-tack.

GROUND RULES

How do people know what is expected of them in a housegroup situation? Is it ever discussed, or do we just pick up clues from each other? You may find it helpful to discuss some ground rules for the housegroup at the start of this course, even if your group has been going a long time. This also gives you an opportunity to talk about how you, as the leader, see the group. Ask everyone to think about what they want to get out of the course. How do they want the group to work? What values do they want to be part of the group's experience; honesty, respect, confidentiality? How do they want their contributions to be treated? You could ask everyone to write down three ground rules on slips of paper and put them in a bowl. Pass the bowl around the group. Each person takes out a rule and reads it, and someone collates the list. Discuss the ground rules that have been suggested and come up with a top five. This method enables everyone to contribute fairly anonymously. Alternatively, if your group are all quite vocal, have a straight discussion about it!

NB Not all questions in each session are covered, some are self-explanatory.

ICONS

 The aim of the session

 Engaging with the world

 Investigate what else the Bible says

 How does this apply to me?

 What about my church?

SESSION 1

MATERIALS NEEDED

A large map of the world that you don't mind stickers being put onto

Small stickers

A pen and paper for everyone in the group

SET THE SCENE

This activity is designed to get people thinking globally. At this stage we are only thinking about our friends who live abroad, and holidays that we've been on. As the book unfolds you will see how to integrate your global awareness with the rest of your life and with the way that you think about church and mission.

These questions are in some ways the questions that the whole of this book seeks to address. We don't expect your group to go into too much depth at this point. Use this exercise to find out what different members in your group think, at this initial stage, about the topic of mission.

1 Lots of Christians, without admitting it, will believe that the only 'real' missionaries are those who are 'full-time' and go abroad. However, when Jesus commissions those present at his ascension to go into all the world and make disciples, he doesn't mention full-time missionaries. Neither does he call some to obey him and others to get on with their work back at home.

   Clearly everyone is not called to dedicate the entirety of their lives to overseas mission, but we should all be involved in this command in some way.

2 Don't probe too deeply; these are just initial ideas. You could mention short term mission, mission on our door step, being involved by financing various projects, writing to those in prison because of their faith etc.

3 People will have an opinion as to what their role in mission is. Give everybody an opportunity to express their opinion. You might want to ask people if they are open for this to be changed throughout the course of this book.

4 If we are more connected today than ever before, then mission to other countries isn't something we need to leave to the few. We can all get involved.

5 Thinking about globalisation should help us to think outside of the box, and see that mission is something we can all do. There are lots of creative ways in which we can be involved; this is both exciting and scary. Throughout this workbook, we will be challenged with change and new ideas. It is up to you and your group how you respond to the difficulties of being challenged by change.

6 The majority of the church, like the majority of the Israelites, want to go back to what they know, to what is more comfortable. Joshua and Caleb saw that the people of Israel had an opportunity before them and so they sought to encourage and inspire the people to stop their cynicism and be a people of hope. The passage doesn't relate directly to the situation or topic we are discussing today, but the responses to change are all too familiar.

WORSHIP
Put the map of the world in the middle of the group and make sure everyone can see it.

SESSION 2

MATERIALS NEEDED

Pens

Large piece of paper and marker pen

FEEDBACK

As people arrive, find out if they remembered to think of any creative ways of doing global mission.

1,2 Circumcision. Making a decision regarding circumcision was hard because it meant respecting a long standing cultural expression of faith and yet being faithful to the gospel of Christ. Essentially what the council were having to do is integrate the Jewish and Christian faiths. A massive shift in thinking needed to take place.

3 The council responded with both sensitivity and integrity. It affirmed that it is by Christ, not circumcision, that people were saved, and yet it asked the Gentile people to respect the long-standing Jewish law over abstaining from certain practices. Their solution was both progressive and pragmatic.

5 The council's response is probably a good one to emulate when thinking about which parts of Christianity and mission are 'absolute' or simply cultural. Some things that are a part of our Christianity are simply cultural and need to be challenged (you can probably think of some examples) but we need to be sensitive and pragmatic in how we challenge the church.

INDIVIDUAL ACTIVITY

The debates about cultural change, and about postmodernity and its characteristics, are endless. It is also worth noting that the differences between modernity and postmodernity are not really as black and white at this exercise makes out. However, as a way into understanding the differences, this exercise is a good start. The important thing to note is that it does not matter whether you think like a modern or a postmodern; both have their advantages and disadvantages. Just be honest.

6 Some people will be more aware of it than others but let everybody express their thoughts on this issue.

8 The issue of whether Christians are affected by culture is a very sensitive one. Few people will deny that we are, but the extent to which we are and should be is an age-old debate. Whether we like it or not we are affected by our culture. Those who are worried about selling out to whatever postmodernity is, might well be reminded that we are already sold out to a modern way of being Christian. Take for example the worship songs we sing and the instrumentation; whether that is with an organ or a band, both are used as a result of the culture around us. What about our businesslike approach to church and church meetings – where has this been adopted from?

9 *Evangelism* – has often been characterised as being about preaching at people, and yet we are increasingly living in a culture when truth is not seen as black and white. A lot of postmodern people need to be taken on a journey of what truth is and gradually they will become involved in the Christian walk. This takes dialogue.

Mission – the increase in gap years, and short term mission.

What is mission – hopefully the influence of postmodernity will enable us to focus more on people and relationships than it will on the number of people we have converted, or with the mission machine that some organisations have created. Mission is partly about building relationships; something actively encouraged by the postmoderns. Postmodernity encourages diversity, and so we can begin to see that we can do mission in all sorts of ways.

WORSHIP
Try and encourage an honesty in your worship. It is always good if the leader sets an example in this. Have you sometimes been too nostalgic, and too cynical about the future? Use this as your springboard into worship.

SESSION 3

MATERIALS NEEDED

Large piece of paper, marker pens

The music for *Beauty for Brokenness*, a copy of the words for everyone – the words and music can be found in *Worship Today*, published by Spring Harvest.

FEEDBACK

Find out if anybody gave any more thought to the question from last week. Don't spend too much time but, whilst you are having coffee, give people the opportunity to share their discoveries.

TO SET THE SCENE

If you are in a particularly big group you might want to split up into smaller groups so that everybody has the opportunity to say what they think. If you do it this way, get each group to share their thoughts when you come back together.

1,2 Often we neglect the commands in the Old Testament regarding justice in the here and now. People have replaced them by concentrating on the justice that we will receive on Judgment Day. Often our fixation with heaven has prevented us from recognising that justice for today's world is important.

3 There is no doubt that the Old Testament focuses on justice in the here and now, but is this replaced or surpassed by new teaching in the New Testament? Jesus is clear that he is seeking for justice in the present (Luke 4). Do these three passages make it legitimate for us to speak of the significance of justice in our mission? We will leave that up to you!

4 Is mission just a couple of these things, or is it all of them? Should we prioritise between the different aspects of mission? We need to steer towards a more holistic approach to mission. This enables us to see mission as something which is not just for the professionals.

WORSHIP

If you have somebody who plays the guitar or keyboard in your group, you can get them to lead you in singing this chorus. If not and you are not confident enough as a group to sing unaccompanied, sing along to a CD, or simply get people to reflect and meditate on the words of the song.

SESSION 4

MATERIALS NEEDED

Bibles

FEEDBACK

Find out if anybody was able to get hold of or read *Intimacy and Involvement*. If so, then ask them to share with the group what they thought of it.

SET THE SCENE

Allow everybody to say what they think about the statement. Make sure that this part of the session is only a short reflection. Get a feel for different people's views on mission and let this guide how you might challenge or encourage the members of your group later in this session, or in another session.

1   Remember a missionary is not just somebody who does full-time overseas missionary work. Maybe you feel like you are not a very good missionary but that doesn't mean you aren't one. We are all called to be mission-minded, and to think globally.

2   We can all do some of these things. Encourage people that thinking globally isn't as hard as it sounds and you really can make a difference.

3   You might want to go through the various passages and identify what gifts each person has. Try to be specific in your encouragement, and don't be typically English and hold back.

4   So many people want to become more like a Billy Graham or a George Verwer. We need to start with the gifts that we have and the person that God has made us, and realise that our mission is not about becoming more like somebody else but more like the person that we are. Mission is a way of life, being yourself whilst bringing the Kingdom of God to people in whatever way suits the person that you are.

WORSHIP

Encourage people to be honest about their insecurities, so that as a group you can pray specifically and give encouragement.

PREPARATION FOR NEXT SESSION

Write down everybody's name on a piece of paper and get them to agree to make or buy a part of the meal for next week. You will probably have to ring round your group during the week to remind them what they agreed to bring.

SESSION 5

PREPARATION BEFORE THE SESSION

Make sure you have set out the table and arranged for everybody to bring some food with them.

MATERIALS NEEDED

Flip chart, or large piece of paper, marker pen

TO SET THE SCENE

Discuss these questions whilst eating the meal. If people have had no direct contact with Christians from other parts of the world, then discuss what you have heard about them. Once you have finished your meal, leave the washing up until afterwards and discuss the rest of the session in another room (otherwise you might lose the momentum of the discussion).

1   We need to work together. Just as a body can't operate properly without all the parts, so a church cannot operate properly without everybody working together. Those who think that they're not good enough to be a part of the body need to be reminded of how important they are. Those who think they can do it all on their own need to be reminded of the importance of other parts of the body.

2   Just as different parts of the world have different dishes, so they have different expressions of church, different resources and different characteristics regarding their spirituality. In the West we are very good at teaching the Bible, and still have much to offer other countries in this respect. However, we have much to learn. For example, churches in the third world have a far more developed understanding of suffering and we would do well to listen to their reflections on this subject. Surely it would be worth our while spending some time being inspired by the church in South America, for example. If their passion and zest for Jesus could rub off on some of us in the West, we would be far richer for it.

3   Maybe your church is quite good at showing a global awareness by supporting and encouraging the church throughout the world. However, most churches show little awareness of the problems that plague Christians in other countries. Does your church have a global focus in its services each week, once a month or not at all? A few members of Crofton Baptist Church in Orpington decided that the global focus of the Sunday services wasn't enough for them and so have started a prayer group for the suffering church, as well as giving time to writing

letters to those in other countries suffering in prison for their faith. Maybe you could do something similar!

4 The fact that we are well educated in the West has both its advantages and disadvantages. Unfortunately, it has given us a teacher complex and meant that often when we do mission, we think we know best. For a long time we have been sceptical about receiving missionaries from other countries. After all, isn't it our job to send and not receive missionaries? We need to start listening again, becoming like the child who is inquisitive and eager to learn.

5 At this stage, any suggestion is valid and the more suggestions the better. You might like to use a flip chart or big sheet of paper to put your ideas on.

6 This is not an opportunity for mindless criticism. Make sure you are sensitive and constructive in the way that you approach the weaknesses of your church.

7 The diagram only gives an overview. If people have more specific examples that help flesh out some of these thoughts, then allow them to share their insight.

SESSION 6

MATERIALS NEEDED

The music for *Let Your Glory Fall (Father of Creation)*, a copy of the words for everyone – words can be found in *Worship Today*, published by Spring Harvest.

FEEDBACK

Give people an opportunity to share their findings. Has anybody made contact with any churches they have connections with?

TO SET THE SCENE

1   Often we are waiting to hear from God before we make our first hesitant steps into a situation of discomfort. Sometimes, however, God requires that we make the first move; be bold and wait for God to respond 'Go and I will be with you.' Peter takes the initiative and Jesus responds by encouraging him to be brave and step out of the boat. This does not mean we don't listen to God, or that we become unnecessarily reckless but sometimes those who wait on the Lord end up waiting forever and never really leave the boat at all.

2   Encourage people to be honest about the sort of person that they are. Are they a risk taker or not? Are they sometimes a little too reckless?

3,4 We are told: 'Immediately Jesus reached out his hand and caught [Peter]'. God promises to be there for us, and if you run into difficulties when you are doing something for him, he will stretch out his arm to save you. But he doesn't always act immediately and sometimes it may seem he doesn't act at all. Let people be honest about their own experiences.

5   Spend some time talking about fear of failure. This is often the one thing that prevents people from ever doing anything. The potential for failure is what makes life an adventure. We come alive when we embrace an adventure beyond our control, or when we walk into a battle we are not sure that we will win.

6,7 These two reflective questions are an opportunity to discuss what you have learnt through the sessions in this book. Use these two questions as a spring board into further discussion. Let people be honest about what they have felt about the sessions. Have the sessions changed people's understanding of God, themselves or others?

WORSHIP

If you have somebody who plays the guitar or keyboard in your group, you can get them to lead you in singing this chorus. If not and you are not confident enough as a group to sing unaccompanied, sing along to a CD, or simply get people to reflect and meditate on the words of the song.

Worship is enriched by silence. Allow yourselves to have a time of quiet reflection when God can challenge you, encourage you and minister to you. Listen for anything you feel he might be saying to you personally, your group, or your church.

FURTHER READING

Globalisation

Thomas Friedman, *The Lexus and the Olive Tree*, (London: Harper Collins, 2000)

Naomi Klein, *No Logo*, (London: Flamingo, 2001)

Tom Sine, *Mustard Seed versus McWorld*, (London: Monarch, 1999)

Postmodernity

Gerard Kelly, *Getting a grip on the future without losing your hold on the past*, (London: Monarch, 1999)

Brian McLaren, *A New Kind of Christian*, (San Francisco: Josey-Bass, 2001)

Jim Powell, *Postmodernism for Beginners*, (London: Writers and Readers, 1998)

Global church

Paul-Gordon Chandler, *God's Global Mosaic*, (Downers Grove: Inter-Varsity Press, 2000)

Patrick Johnstone, *Operation World 21st Century Edition*, (Carlisle: Paternoster Lifestyle with WEC International, 2001)

Ronald Sider, *Rich Christians in an Age of Hunger*, (London: Hodder & Stoughton, 1978)

Short term mission

Cathie Bartlam, *Mind the Gap – true stories of year-out projects*, (Milton Keynes: Scripture Union, 1999)

ORGANISATIONS YOU MIGHT FIND HELPFUL INCLUDE

Global Connections

Whitefield House, 186 Kennington Park Road, London, SE11 4BT

– they publish *Global Connections Code of Best Practice in Short-term Mission*.

Tel: 020 7207 2156

Email: info@globalconnections.co.uk

Christian Vocations

Tel: 01384 233511

Web: www.christianvocations.org

Oasis

Email: enquiries@oasistrust.org

Web: www.oasistrust.org

Tel: 0207 450 9000